ROCKABE

Classic Edition

Written by Kelly Polark
Illustrated by Kelli Ann Little

ISBN: 0988846276
ISBN-13: 978-0988846272

My kids rock!
This is for Josh, Em, & Jack. -   KP

A is for Aerosmith,
Their first hit, "Dream On."

B is for the Beatles,
George, Ringo, Paul, John.

C is for the Cars.
They like nightlife, baby.

D - that's the Doors
Who "Love Her Madly."

E is for Elvis,
The Rock 'n' Roll King.

F - **Fleetwood Mac**
"Dreams" they can sing.

G is G N' R.
They've got fun and games.

H is for Hendrix
Who rocked "Purple Haze."

I - Billy Idol
He cried for more.

J is Joan Jett
Plus the Runaways four.

K is for Kiss.
They shout it loud.

L - Lynyrd Skynyrd
"Free Bird" for the crowd.

M - Mötley Crüe
They kickstart your heart.

N is Nirvana,
Sang "Come as You Are."

O - **Ozzy Osbourne**
He barks at the moon.

P is Pat Benatar.
"We Belong" is her tune.

Q is for Queen.
Their anthems will rock you.

R - Rolling Stones
Jagger's moves may shock you.

S is Skid Row.
Oh, "I Remember You."

T is Tom Petty
And the Heartbreakers, too.

U is for U2
Enjoying a "Beautiful Day."

V - that's Van Halen.
Let's "Dance the Night Away."

W is for Winger
Who are "Hungry" like you.

X is INXS.
They "Taste It," too.

Y is for the Yardbirds,
Starring Beck, Clapton, Page.

Z is for Led Zeppelin
with "Black Dog" onstage.

About the Author:

Kelly Polark is a mom of three who is a grade school teacher and author from the Midwest. She is a contributor to *Spider*, *Ladybug*, and *Highlights Puzzlemania* magazines. She is the author of two MeeGenius digital picture books: BIG SISTER, BABY BROTHER and HOLD THE MUSTARD! She also wrote WORDS ON BIRDS and I'M A LITTLE GREEN WITCH. Her debut middle grade novel is titled ROCK 'N' ROLL PRINCESSES WEAR BLACK. In her free time, Kelly hangs with her family, reads books, and sings along at rock concerts. Check out her website, BOOK RECS OF THE ROCK AND FAMOUS (www.bookrecsthatrock.blogspot.com). Please say stop and say hey on Facebook (www.facebook.com/AuthorKellyPolark) and Twitter (@kellypolark), too!

About the Illustrator:

Kelli Ann is a mom of two (a mustang named Rambo and a chameleon named Thor) and set to graduate Western State Colorado University in the spring of 2014. ROCKABET is her first published work, and she is currently working on another title she hopes to get out soon. She enjoys long trail rides in the mountains and loves a good starry sky. Both a self-proclaimed film freak and animation snob, Kelli is also a comic enthusiast and hopes to break into that field in the near future. More of her personal work and an up-to-date portfolio can be found at her Facebook (facebook.com/catching.dreamz) and her Deviantart account (catching-dreamz.deviantart.com).

♫

Printed in Great Britain
by Amazon